Until Death...

Judith Hall Shelton

Until Death

Copyright © 2021 by Judith Hall Shelton

All rights reserved. No part of this book may be reproduced or transmitted in any form or by any means without written permission from the author.

Scripture is used from the NKJV

ISBN 9798473333046

Printed in USA by 48HrBooks (www.48HrBooks.com)

Dedication

To the memory of the man who loved me when I was unlovable. The man who chose me above all others to be his wife and the mother of his children. He was my first and greatest true love. In honor of my three precious children, my sweet grandchildren and great-grand children who were never blessed to know the man I loved so much.

Thank you to my wonderful friend and neighbor, Brenda Kent, who was gracious enough to edit this book. Even though the story was written many years ago, she was the first to read this revised and most current edition. Thank You God for blessing me with such a sweet friend.

Thank you to Dorothy Gates who guided me through the process of getting this book published. She encouraged me to push on when at times I wanted to put it down and quit. God bless you Dorothy.

Introduction

Have you ever asked God "Why?" certain things happen to you? "Why can't I be as successful, as wealthy, as happy as others around me?"

God has a *perfect will* for our lives and a *permissive will*. His perfect will for us is to follow the plan He has laid out for our lives. What He wants us to do and who He wants us to be. He has, however, given us the option of choice. He never forces us to do or be anything we choose not to be. We are free to choose the path we take. This is where choice comes in. We can choose to follow His perfect will, or we can choose to go our own way. Upon doing so we are also choosing the consequences of our actions. This does not mean He will not bless us in our choices, but our blessings will not compare to those of His *perfect will.*

In my heart I believe a decision made to follow a wrong path many, many years ago, not by me, may have led to some tragedies that affected my life as I grew up. I cannot place blame for all my life's problems on that one decision, however, in many cases it was my wrong choices that led me away from God's *perfect will* and into His *permissive will.*

Our choices in life not only affect us but those who come after us...our children, grandchildren and generations to come.

If you have never accepted Christ as your Savior, please do so now. Then pray for God to show and guide you into His perfect will for your life. When you are tempted to go down a path that looks fun and inviting but out of His will, ask Him for strength to stay on the right path of His *Perfect Will*. You will never regret this "choice."

Until Death

"Do you, Judie, take Hayes to be your lawfully wedded husband; to love, honor and cherish him from this day forward, for better or worse, in sickness and in health...until death...until death...until death......"

As I sat in the intensive care waiting room of North Mississippi Medical Center listening to the words the doctor was saying, my head began to roar, my heart felt as though it would burst, and more than twenty-one years of my life raced through my mind.

We were young and so much in love when Hayes and I married. Twenty years into the future seemed like an eternity to us. We lived each day to the fullest just loving each other and never really worrying about tomorrow. There was very little money and by the time our bills were paid, sometimes we had less than $0.50 to last us all week. But we were appreciative of what we had. Most of all we had each other.

There were good times and bad times. Somehow even some of the bad times as years went by began to seem not so bad. For example, there was the time in October 1959 while we were living at Beacon Hill and Hayes was working for MFC on highway 15. He only brought home about $35 a week. We were paying $75 a month rent plus utilities. Our first baby was due in about two months. One morning I got up to cook breakfast before Hayes went to work only to find out we didn't have any propane gas. We didn't have enough money to have the tank filled so for the next three days we ate cold cereal for breakfast. For supper we had pork-n-beans and wieners heated for a couple hours in front of an electric heater. Hayes was laughing at work telling the guys how I was cooking supper. One of his bosses apparently felt sorry for us and invited us to his home for supper on Friday night. I don't think fried chicken, potatoes and gravy had ever tasted so good! It was hard, but we tried not to act starved. Years later we laughed about this experience.

The house we lived in sat up off the highway looking down on a small motel. To us it seemed almost like a mansion. The floors were hardwood except in the kitchen/dining room and the bathroom. We had two bedrooms, a big living room, large kitchen/dining area, one bathroom and a carport. We lived in the house approximately a month and had company every day or night except one.

As I said, our money was scarce and with a baby on the way we began looking for a smaller, less expensive place. Also, we weren't sure just how many more trips our old Studebaker would be able to make it up the steep driveway. We found and rented a one-bedroom furnished apartment in New Albany. The evening we went to move in the landlord told us the mobile home we had asked about had been vacated that day. He had not had time to clean it but if we were still interested, we could have it for the same price as the apartment. We gladly took it and moved in that night.

I wasn't much of a cook, but we stayed healthy in spite of it. Our evening meals consisted mainly of fried potatoes or cream-style corn, fried streak 'o lean or fatback (generously furnished by Hayes' folks), cornbread, and when I managed to get them done without burning them, black-eyed peas. Our bedtime snack was most often canned biscuits or cornbread and buttermilk, which we also got from Hayes' parents.

The autumn nights were getting cooler, but the days were filled with a hint of the lingering summer. There was excitement in the air as the arrival of our baby was approaching and we made plans to build a home. We could only afford a shell home, but it was going to be ours. Hayes was the type of person who could do almost anything he wanted to do-- carpentry, plumbing, electrical work--and the list goes on. Naturally we would save money by finishing the inside of our home ourselves. I think Mr. Charlie, Hayes' dad, was almost as excited about the house as we were. He couldn't wait for the carpenters to get started so he could see the job well done.

Late in November we spent a weekend in Memphis looking at houses and talking to sales representatives. I was beginning to feel pretty sick by the end of the day Saturday. The baby seemed so low and my stomach and back ached. I didn't want Hayes to know because I knew he would be worried about me and want to go home. I just toughed it out trudging from one place to another looking. Late Sunday evening we started home. I knew the baby wasn't due for about three weeks, but I certainly was feeling miserable. Oh well, I thought I was just tired.

After we arrived home a salesman from Atlas Shell Homes and his wife came over. We discussed plans for the home we wanted to build until after midnight. For some reason I couldn't sit flat in a chair. I kept twisting and turning, sitting first on one leg then the other. I ached all over but was sure I would feel better after a good night's rest. Well, that was not to happen!!

Not long after having gone to sleep I began waking up having these strange pains in my back and the lower part of my stomach. I was so green or maybe naive I just knew it wasn't time for the baby to come. By six o'clock Monday morning I was almost twisting holes in Hayes' t-shirt every time I had a pain. Finally, we decided we better go to the hospital even though they would probably send me back home--but they didn't.

After a very long day of pain and grogginess from the shots I had been given, we finally had our beautiful new baby girl. We named her Judith Ann. I don't believe any father has ever been prouder of a baby than Hayes was of Judith Ann. She had a head full of black hair and a little round face. Naturally she was the most beautiful baby in the nursery! Hayes spent most of his time at the hospital showing her off to anyone he could corner and head toward the nursery.

"Hold up my baby, the one with all the pretty black hair!" he would say to the nurses. *"I want these folks to see that she looks just like her Daddy."*

The day we took our little doll home from the hospital to Grandmother's, Mr. Charlie went to the store and bought a tin can of Mennen's baby powder, safety pins, and socks big enough for a two-year-old to wear. Mrs. Hall said it was the first time he had ever bought presents for a grandbaby. He would kneel down beside the bed and call her Granddaddy's little heart. Our little girl was only about two months old when Mr. Charlie died, and we moved in with Mrs. Hall. She was very partial to Judith Ann because Granddaddy had loved her so much.

Soon it was spring. We were offered a job with Myrtle Telephone Company. I was to be the operator and Hayes would do all the installations and repairs. We would be furnished a place to live and later on a vehicle. Our salary would be $275 a month and I would be working right at home. After quite a bit of discussion we decided to take the job and on June 1, 1960 we moved out of Mrs. Hall's house into the one where the telephone exchange was. Being an operator, even in such a small town, was a twenty-four-hour job seven days a week. Of course, we both learned to operate the switchboard. Hayes would stay with it one day a week so I could go to the grocery store. We never had a chance to go anywhere together. A few months later we taught Hayes' sister, Virginia, to operate the switchboard and also a young couple down the street so someone would be available if we ever had an emergency. During the summer of 1960 my sister Karen came to live with us. She was only seven years old. Just a short while before my brother, Wayne, had also come to live with us. He was going to be a senior in high school that fall.

Each of them learned how to answer the phone and make calls for customers so my job became less demanding of my time. At least I could wash and hang out clothes or cook a full meal without having to run back and forth to the switchboard.

In February we found out that we were going to get another little bundle of joy. My how our family was growing. We were counting on this one being a boy and sure enough on October 30th we got our handsome baby boy. We named him Ronald Allen and decided to call him Ronnie. He was just twenty-three months and seven days younger than his big sister. He didn't have as much hair as she had when she was born. However, Daddy was just as proud of him as he had been of Ronnie's big sister. Our little girl was the image of the Halls. Except for his eyes, our little boy favored me, his mother. Of course, I thought this was great!

Now there were six of us living on less than $300 a month. Wayne worked enough to make a little spending money for himself. Times were hard but in spite of it all we were happy and didn't really want for anything.

Hayes always saw to it that his bills were paid, and his family's needs met.

Along about this time integration was taking place in the south. Hayes was serving in the National Guard. When the first black student attempted to enroll at the University of Mississippi (Ole Miss) in Oxford, a small war broke out in that small college town. The National Guard was called out and sent to Oxford to help keep the peace. Regular Army men from many parts of the United States were also deployed to Oxford.

For a week or more after the guardsmen were sent to Oxford family members were not allowed to visit them. Finally though, peace was restored, and we were permitted to go for a visit one Sunday afternoon. The guard squadron of which Hayes was a member was bivouacked in a field south of Oxford. I fried chicken and fixed all the trimmings for a picnic lunch. It seemed as though Hayes had been there for months. We were all excited to go see Daddy. During our visit a reporter from the

Memphis Commercial Appeal came by and took our picture. The following week it appeared in the paper and we felt like celebrities. The caption read…"Cpl. Hayes Hall and his family enjoy a leisurely afternoon visit amongst turmoil".

The kids did not go with me the second time I visited Hayes. It was on a weeknight and I went with two or three other women whose husbands were in the guard. By this time the New Albany squadron had been moved to the Ole Miss football field. I never knew why, but for some reason Hayes did not seem glad to see me. He got upset when I told him a young man had come from Louisiana to do telephone repair work while he was away. It seemed as if it made him angry that his sister Virginia and Jimmy were taking care of the kids and the switchboard that night so I could come visit him. For the rest of the evening, he kept his back toward me and wouldn't talk to me. I even heard one of the other guys say Hayes had a different visitor nearly every night. I was disturbed over it but decided later he acted that way because he was tired and under a lot of stress. After twenty-eight days the guardsmen were allowed to come home to their families.

During the time Hayes served in the National Guard he spent one weekend a month on duty at the Armory and two weeks each summer in Hattiesburg at Camp Shelby, MS. In 1962 there was another incident that seemed strange at the time. Hayes had been to summer camp for two weeks. It was Sunday, Hayes was expected to be home about noon and I was cooking things I knew he liked. About ten minutes before he got there his friend Chip came over to see what time he would be home. He was going back to Memphis but wanted to see Hayes first. As we stood in the kitchen talking Hayes drove up. Naturally we both went out to meet him. Hayes just looked at me and didn't say a word but began talking to Chip. It was not until several months later during an argument he mentioned the incident. I couldn't believe he was making those insinuations. I tried to explain but he wouldn't listen. Finally, he said, *"Okay, just forget it!"*

Early in 1963 we found out that as a result of our love for each other we were once again going to be blessed with another precious little newcomer. This time we had no preference as to the sex of the baby. We just wanted our new baby to be healthy. We decided this would be the last addition to our family. We believed that with the help of God if we could bring up our children to be responsible, dependable citizens we could say we had succeeded in life. We also had the responsibility of my youngest sister so, in a sense, we would have four children to rear with God's help. On October 3rd our second precious baby boy was born. We named him Charles David after two of Hayes' brothers. As it had been with the other two babies, Hayes was very proud of his new baby son. God had been so wonderful to bless us with three beautiful, healthy children.

Progress was reaching into the small town of Myrtle. Changes were taking place and leading the pack was none other than Myrtle Telephone Company. Finally dial phones were going to replace the old crank phones of the past. After three years of twenty-four hours a day, seven days a week it was almost as though we were going to be out of prison. We would be able to go places together. We could sit down and eat a meal without being interrupted by phone calls. We could go to church together, visit friends, or watch television without being interrupted. Our bedroom would no longer be in the living room with the switchboard. However, the thing that excited us the most was that now we would finally be able to move into our home. By this time, we had already outgrown it and would immediately have to begin adding on. We had waited almost three years and at last our dream was about to become reality!! On May 1, 1963 we moved in. It wasn't big or fancy, but it was OURS and we were so proud of it!

We added another bedroom and bathroom and remodeled the kitchen. Soon the construction was finished, and we were all settled in. Hayes was working very hard every day putting up phone cable, installing new phones and learning all he could about the office equipment. He caught on quickly and in no time at all he had everything running smoothly and was put completely in charge of the new Myrtle Telephone Company.

For a number of years things went relatively smooth. We had the usual problems all young married couples have but always managed to work them out together. We began going to church regularly again when Bro. David Poe came to pastor Temple Baptist Church. He and his wife became two of our dearest friends, as did Billy and Frances Basil. We went on picnics together, camping trips, had cookouts and visited each other as often as possible. It wasn't unusual for us to have fifteen or twenty people at our house for a fish fry, grilled steaks or grilled hamburgers. One night I remember almost as if it were last week, we decided to have a big fish fry. We invited about forty people. Since our house was small, we got permission to use the agriculture building at the school so everyone could be inside if it rained. The Willards brought their guitars and when everyone had finished eating, they entertained us with a little picking and grinning. Both Hayes and I enjoyed being with our friends, so we had company or visited often.

Being a good wife and mother had always been important to me. I had a full-time job taking care of our home and three children. For this reason, Hayes had never wanted me to work outside our home. However, after working for the phone company for about seven years, the pressure of the job seemed to be getting to Hayes. He began to feel like it was time for him to find some other kind of work. Of course, a job change would put a strain on our finances. After much discussion and prayer, we decided that I would go to college, get my degree in elementary education and teach school. A woman with children in school couldn't ask for a better job...in our opinion. Mrs. Hall agreed to baby-sit David so I could attend Blue Mountain College. The other two children and Karen were in school. It wouldn't be necessary for me to be gone all day so I could still do my housework and be home when the kids came home from school. Hayes began doing a little carpenter work in his spare time. Almost before we knew it three years had passed; I had my BS degree in elementary education and would soon be teaching at Myrtle.

In the fall of 1969, I began teaching fifth grade. I was so excited!! Every morning the kids and I got dressed and went to school together. Every afternoon we came home together. When they were out for holidays and summer vacation, I could be with them. I loved my job and tried to do my best.

Before the end of my first year of teaching I was asked if I would be interested in taking a position as remedial reading teacher the following year. It meant I would have to go back to college for a while, but it was also an opportunity for me to get my Master's Degree. Also, I would have to agree to stay in the Chapter 1 program long enough for it to be worth the county paying my tuition. Before making a decision, I discussed it with Hayes and together we decided it was what I should do. In the summer of 1970, I started attending classes at Ole Miss. Two and a half summers later I completed my Master's Degree with a Specialization in Reading.

By 1973 Hayes was doing carpenter work full time. His nerves seemed to be more settled since he quit working for the telephone company. God had been very good to us and we were happy. We purchased a small camper and a pick-up truck and began camping as often as we could. Later we built a very nice camper and purchased a special pick-up to haul it. We named our camper "Hall-A-Way" because we were the Halls and could "haul" it away anytime and almost anywhere we wanted.

We loved traveling, especially into the Smoky and Ozark Mountains. It was on one of these trips that our tragedy began. We had traveled more than 2000 miles from home to the Smokies; to West Virginia to visit my relatives on my Mother's side; to Niagara Falls; to Aurora, IL to visit with members of Hayes' family; St. Louis, MO to see the Cardinals play baseball; and on to Memphis to visit Hayes' sister and her family.

While at Dorothy's, Hayes and I were in the camper resting and loving each other when he said, *"I just had the strangest thing happen to me. I have this tingling sensation all over and I saw the image of a guy I knew in the National Guard. I could see his face and he was just smiling at me. Now I smell something like ether."*

The sensation only lasted for a few seconds. We talked about it for quite a while then decided he was tired and nervous from the trip, especially all the driving. But we were wrong! The same thing happened again after we got home and as time went on the sensations became more frequent and began to change. Hayes went to our family doctor, but he couldn't find any physical problems that may be causing the "spells", as we began to call them, to happen. He suggested that maybe there was cause for some psychiatric treatment. The mention of this really upset Hayes. However, our doctor prescribed a mild nerve tablet he thought would help. The tablets only worked for a short period of time. The spells or seizures gradually became more and more frequent.

One morning in February of 1975 I was called to the school office. Our neighbor, Rev. Raymond Bishop, was waiting there for me. I knew immediately something was wrong, but I was afraid to ask. My heart was pounding, and I felt as though I could not breathe.

"Hayes called to me as I was passing your house a while ago," he began. *"He said he was sick. I don't know if he is having a heart attack or not. He's complaining of hurting*

really bad in his back and chest. I think you should go home."

Mr. Hood, our school principal, agreed so I gathered up my things and Bro. Bishop took me home. I found Hayes in severe pain, walking the floor. About 12:30 p.m. I convinced him to let me take him to the doctor who after examining him sent him to the hospital for x- rays and an electrocardiogram. At the emergency room the staff was treating Hayes as though he had a heart attack. He kept telling them he was hurting in his back worse than in his chest. He was admitted to the hospital and shortly after he said to me, *"I dreamed I had one of those spells today and it was a really bad one."*

Bro. Danny Bryant, our pastor at that time, came to the hospital almost immediately when I called to tell him Hayes was there. He was a Cub Scout leader and was dressed to go to a Scout banquet that night. Several times he mentioned he needed to leave so he would not be late for the banquet but for some reason kept sitting there. As I think back now, I realize God was keeping him there.

About 6:00 p.m., as the three of us were talking, Hayes began to look very strange. His body began to draw, and his eyes rolled back in his head. Immediately I called for the nurse. I was hysterical because I thought he was dying. Within a matter of seconds, the room was filled with nurses and doctors. As they began working with Hayes someone took me out of the room to the nurses' lounge.

"God please don't let him die! Please don't take him away from me," I prayed. *"Dear God, I can't live without him!"*

It seemed like hours passed before the doctor finally came to the nurses' lounge where I had been waiting. The tablet I was given to calm me down had just begun to take effect when the doctor came in. My heart was pounding so hard in my ears I could hardly hear, and my stomach was tied in knots. I wanted to say, "How is he?", but the words would not come out.

Understanding my concern, the doctor quickly said, *"Hayes is okay. He had a grand mal seizure and will sleep for a while. You can go back in and be with him now."* Thank God my love had not been taken from me! My prayer had been answered.

That night as my husband slept, I knelt by the cot in his room and thanked God again for not taking my love away from me. Also, I prayed, *"God please, please don't let Hayes have any more convulsions like the ones he had today."* While I was still on my knees a calm feeling came over me. I knew God had given me the assurance that my prayer was answered.

What Hayes had thought was a dream earlier that day had been reality. The places where he had bitten his tongue and the overturned lamp in the living room were now like pieces of a puzzle finally falling into place. How terrible it must have been for him to go through it alone!

For the next three- or four-days Hayes was given muscle relaxers and pain killers. He kept telling the doctor and nurses he was having a lot of pain in his back. Each time anyone woke him up he had muscle spasms in his back and chest. Finally, on Tuesday he convinced the doctor there was something wrong with his back. More x-rays were made, and these showed three compressed vertebrae in his upper spine. Arrangements were made for us to go to North Mississippi Medical Center in Tupelo the next day. The trip was rough on Hayes. Every little movement caused more spasms in his back. Time seemed to drag, and he was suffering so much, but finally he was settled into a room.

Nearly a week of x-rays, brain scans, and other tests followed. No apparent reason for the convulsions could be found. The only explanation given was possibly epilepsy. He was fitted with a brace, placed on medication, which included phenobarbital for the control of the seizures, and was released from the hospital.

For approximately a year Hayes wore the back brace. Muscle spasms were frequent day and night. Many nights he needed pain medication just so he could rest. The mild seizures returned and even though he was taking the prescribed medication, they could not be controlled. Hayes was very upset over this and often expressed fear that he would have another grand mal seizure. I knew he would not because God had assured me of it when he was in the hospital in New Albany. However, he lived in constant fear that it would happen again when he was home alone. Tranquilizers were prescribed for his nerves and medication to relieve the periods of depression he was experiencing.

Each worked for a short period of time then something stronger was needed. For a long time, Hayes took Talwin tablets for pain.

Because they relieved the tension at the same time, he thought they also helped to control the seizures. Therefore, he began taking more tablets more often. Eventually they no longer eased the pain, so the doctor prescribed Talwin injections. I was horrified at the thought of giving a shot but learned to do so in order to help him get some relief. As had been the case with the tablets the shots became more and more frequent and the amount of the dosage increased. One day when the Talwin was gone sooner than it should have been I realized Hayes was giving himself shots when I wasn't home and even when I was. I was shocked and it really bothered me that he needed so many injections. I had learned recently that he was taking the Talwin tablets also. Our druggist became concerned about this problem. It began getting difficult for Hayes to obtain the prescriptions he wanted and now needed. He changed doctors and druggists several times. We started going to the hospital emergency room at night so he could get a shot. His complaint was always back pain. By this time two years had passed and the doctor in Tupelo told us the vertebrae should no longer be causing the severe pain Hayes said he was having. He released Hayes and would no longer see him as his patient. However, the "pain" continued and the trips to the emergency room became more frequent until at last we were going every night and sometimes twice a night. One of the nurses told me they were no longer giving him the pain medicine but a "sugar shot".

His family, many of his friends, and I realized Hayes had a very serious problem. We tried talking to him, but he wouldn't listen. *"Nothing is wrong with me,"* he would say.

Sometimes he'd get very angry and occasionally became violent with our children and me. He began accusing me of taking his medicine and later still of giving it to our daughter. I could not for the life of me understand what was happening to him, to us, to our marriage and our family. We had always been close but now there was a gap between us that could not be crossed.

Everything was falling apart. Our love making became almost non-existent. The quarrels became more frequent and more heated. I began to feel as if I was going crazy. No matter what I did it was wrong. Hayes lost his temper at the least things. I never knew when I said something if it was going to make him angry. I dreaded going home in the afternoons and for the weekends to come because I never knew what to expect next. Our daughter got married and our two sons stayed away from the house as much as possible because they didn't want to see their daddy in a drugged state of mind almost all the time.

There were times when things were good and my hope that we were on the right track again was renewed. Each of these times only turned into bitter disappointment as I watched my love gradually slipping away from me. I felt more hurt than I had ever thought was possible to feel. I began building a wall inside. I convinced myself I didn't care because if I didn't the heartache, I was experiencing wouldn't be so bad. Our children experienced this same hurt because they could not depend on their daddy to be there when they needed him. One incident in particular that comes to mind is when Ronnie was planning to get married. There were so many questions he wanted and needed to ask his daddy but was unable to do so because of his condition. One day Ronnie looked at me and said, *"Mama I need daddy more now than I ever have and he can't help me."*

I thought my heart would break. It was apparent that the children were hurting just as much as I was, if not more. I knew something had to be done, but what? A number of people told me Hayes should be put in a hospital for treatment, but he refused to go. He could "work things out on his own". Friends, doctors, ministers and family members all talked to Hayes but to no avail. He refused to let anyone help, insisting that we were all making a big deal out of nothing.

Over the years since his trouble first began, Hayes had undergone several batteries of tests trying to determine what was causing his problems. There seemed to be no apparent reason for his actions. Everyone came to the conclusion that he was having psychiatric problems coupled with drug abuse.

David was working at Kentucky Fried Chicken after school till closing time. One evening the hospital called. David had cut his hand at work and needed some stitches. It was necessary that I fill out and sign some insurance forms before he could be treated. Hayes said, *"Good, I'll go with you and get a shot while we're there."* I know he didn't mean it the way it sounded but this statement hurt deeply.

Another similar incident took place when Ronnie suffered a mild concussion in a skating accident. Again, when I told Hayes I was going to the hospital he decided he would go along and get a shot *"just to save what he had at the house"*. At the hospital he appeared to be more concerned about himself than he was our son. This was almost more than I could take. Hayes insisted that he be the one to stay at the hospital with Ronnie that night, but I refused. He became angry with me but by this time I was so hurt and furious with him I no longer cared. He finally agreed to let the other kids take him home. Early the next morning Hayes was back to spend the day so I could go to work. Ronnie's girlfriend had also come to stay, and Ronnie told his daddy he didn't need him to stay because she would be there. But this time Hayes could not be persuaded to leave. Around 1:00 p.m. that afternoon I got a phone call from a friend who worked at the hospital.

"Mrs. Hall", said the voice on the other end of the line, *"could you come pick Hayes up? He passed out or went to sleep while eating his lunch in the hospital cafeteria and almost fell out of his chair. We've taken him back up to your son's room but feel like he would be better off at home."*

"Yes, I'll be there as soon as I can," I answered.

Mr. Hood took me to the hospital and told me if I needed any help feel free to call. By the time I reached the hospital Hayes was in a nasty mood. He was sure there had been no need for anyone to call me because he was fine! When I suggested that maybe he should go home because he could rest better there, he jumped up out of his chair, grabbed his coat and said, *"Okay, let's go!!"*

I wasn't about to ride back to Myrtle with him in the condition he was in but didn't know how I was going to go about getting his truck keys from him. As we went down the elevator, I prayed that somehow God would take care of everything. Just as we walked out of the hospital Hayes reached into his pocket and handed me the keys. Once again God had answered prayer for me.

On the way home he looked at me and said, *"Y'all made a fool of me today and I won't forget it. You are going to pay for it. I will get even with you and whoever called you from the hospital."*

By the time we reached the house I knew I could not stand anymore. No longer could I take the accusations and uncertainty that faced me each day. My nerves were almost to the breaking point. I had fought for my husband and my marriage every way I knew how. Now I only had one choice left. I had to leave in the hope that if he really cared about the kids and me, he would get the professional help he so desperately needed and once again we could be a happy family.

On that cold February afternoon as I walked out the front door of our home I didn't know if I would ever be coming back. During the few minutes it took for me to walk to the school almost our whole life together passed before me--all the good times we had going to church together, going camping, raising our children, visiting friends and much more. My heart was breaking for the one I loved so much. **Why did our life together have to**

come to this?? Why wouldn't God just reach down and make everything right for us again?? Why God, why????

"Oh God," I prayed, *"what am I going to do, what am I going to do???"*

By the time I reached Mr. Hood's office I could no longer hold back the river of tears that flowed from my heart. I cried like I had not done for a long, long time.

For the next month I lived with my sister-in-law, Sarah. Hayes was bitter about my leaving at first. He would not come around me and I was afraid to go to our house. Ronnie and David kept a check on him and brought me things I needed from the house. About three weeks after I left Hayes called me one evening. He wanted me to come over and read the Bible to him. Sarah would not let me go alone. We went together and I spent almost two hours reading to Hayes. His mood had begun to change. He was not bitter now, except when he asked me to come back home and I told him I wouldn't until he decided to do something about getting off the drugs.

When he realized I meant business, Hayes began to make a serious effort (still on his own) to change the way things were. On March 13, 1980 just one month from the day I had left, I moved back home. I believed he was headed in the right direction and my place was by his side helping in every way I knew how. The vows we took on our wedding day had been "for better or worse, in sickness and health, until death!

For a short while everything went well. I believed this time we were going to make it. Then gradually the situation returned to the way it had been before. I refused, so Hayes drove himself to the hospital at night to get shots. I was determined I was not going to help him kill himself any longer.

One Saturday late in 1980 Hayes had been gone most of the afternoon. It was about

10:30 p.m. when the phone rang. The voice on the other end of the line said, *"Mrs. Hall, this is a deputy at the jail. We wanted to let you know we have Hayes over here. He apparently has had too much to drink and tried to start some trouble down around West Union. He's okay but he will have to stay here overnight.*

I questioned the deputy as to where his truck and keys were because I didn't want it left sitting somewhere overnight. Ronnie and I went to the jail to get the keys and I heard Hayes yelling inside. I looked up and saw him through one of the downstairs windows. Oh, how I wished I could take him home and somehow make everything alright! My feelings at that moment were a mixture of love and hate for the man I was seeing inside that jail cell. With God giving me strength, I choked back the tears and walked away. It was one of the hardest things I had ever done.

The next morning, I picked Sarah up around 9:00 and we went to the jail to get

Hayes. I couldn't bear the thought of going there alone. I wanted to cry, scream, or run just as far as I could but I knew I couldn't. The tears that seemed so often to fill my eyes these days came again. I tried hard to hold them back. I couldn't break down--not now when it was so necessary to be strong. The charges against Hayes were dropped on his promise that he was going to straighten up and get everything worked out. And the cycle continued. Once again, he refused to seek professional help and his promises were only kept for a few days.

One Sunday morning in the summer of 1980 David and I went to church and left Hayes in bed asleep. When we got home around noon he was not there. All day I waited for him to come home but he didn't. I was worried because I didn't know where he was or what kind of condition, he was in. About 5:30 p.m. he called. *"Can you come over here and get me?"* he asked. *"I'm at the jail and they won't let me go until someone signs my bail."*

All the way to town I felt the same hurt, anger, and sick feeling I had felt so often in the past few years. I was almost afraid to ask what had happened this time.

On the ride home he explained that while driving into town he had crossed the centerline *"just a little bit"* and caused a man to run off the road. The man had turned around followed him to the drugstore, parked behind his truck and called the police. Hayes was sure everyone was making a big deal out of nothing. This time the charges were not dropped, and Hayes had to appear in court in two weeks on a DUI charge. I was embarrassed and humiliated. Why did he insist on doing these things? How much more could we all stand?

The appearance at the court hearing was a terrible experience…for me anyway. Hayes wouldn't plead guilty because it would mean a trial, hiring a lawyer, and bringing up things he wanted kept quiet. He wouldn't plead guilty because he insisted, he wasn't. Finally, the judge continued his case until a later date so he could decide what he wanted to do. He decided to pay the bond money and never made his appearance in court at all.

Late in October I came home from school on Wednesday and found Hayes asleep. When he woke up, I realized at once he was under the influence of phenobarbital to the extent, he was drunk. As the evening turned into night, he got worse. David got very upset and began to cry. *"Mama,"* he said *"if you don't put daddy in the hospital I'm going to leave. I can't take it anymore."* My heart was broken for my baby son!

I knew something had to be done. My children, especially David because the other two were married by now, were suffering and I didn't want this to happen. I called the hospital and asked for an ambulance to be sent to pick Hayes up. I knew he probably would refuse to go so the ER technician suggested I call the sheriff's office and ask them to send a deputy out to the house. When Hayes saw the uniformed officer, he put up no resistance and allowed them to put him in the ambulance and take him to the hospital. During the three days he was in the hospital the doctor regulated his medication and cautioned him about taking too much phenobarbital or he would kill himself or someone else.

The following Tuesday, which was in November, I came home from school and again found Hayes asleep on the bed. As soon as he awoke, I knew he had taken another overdose of medication. The next day was the same. Again, I called for an ambulance to take him to the hospital and called the sheriff's office for back-up and support. Due to the fact he had not offered resistance the other time the sheriff's office didn't think it was necessary to send someone this time. Forty-five minutes after the ambulance arrived, we were still waiting for an officer and Hayes was refusing to go to the hospital. I got so upset I called Sarah, his sister. She called the sheriff's office and explained that if it had not been necessary, I would not have called them. Finally, a deputy showed up but before they got there Ronnie convinced his daddy that he would have to go to jail if he didn't go to the hospital.

This time the doctor agreed to send Hayes to a neurologist in Tupelo for tests in order to keep him in the hospital for a while. Also, we believed if we could get him straightened out eventually, he would agree to talk to a psychiatrist. Friday afternoon we headed to North Mississippi Medical Center.

On Monday he was given the same battery of tests he had been given before with one addition. This time a CT scan, a test that had not been available in the past, was done. The report from this scan was not good. There was a growth of some type on the right side of his brain above his ear. Surgery would be necessary in order to determine the type and seriousness of the tumor. Medication was necessary for at least a week before surgery to reduce swelling in the area. I could not let

Hayes face the next few days alone. He was so scared, like a little boy in many ways, although he tried not to show it. I made arrangements to be off work until after Thanksgiving so I could be with him until surgery was over and we knew everything was going to be alright.

The words I heard screamed loudly in my ears--- *"A malignancy, we couldn't get it all!!!!"*

"Oh God!! Why him?? We've only just begun to live! WHY? WHY? OH GOD I CAN'T STAND THIS." my heart screamed!! *"What am I going to do?? How can I face him knowing what I know? God, please help me, help us!!! Give me strength! The kids!! Someone call the kids! I want them here with us! How am I going to tell them?? Oh God, why couldn't it have been me??"* I cried harder than I had since losing my mother in a car accident when I was 14 years old!! My heart was breaking!!!

The flood of tears I had been holding back for so long all seemed to come at once. I thought I would never stop crying! *"But I have to stop before the kids get here,"* I thought. *"I can't let them see me like this. I have to be strong for them and for my husband!"* Bro. Bob Watkins, our pastor, had been at the hospital with me all day. He prayed with me that night that I would be strong and could accept whatever was in store for my family and me.

That night and the next day Hayes was in intensive care. The hours dragged between visitation times and I knew he felt very alone there. He was moved into a room late afternoon and I could be with him all the time. Although he continued to have quite a bit of pain for several days the doctors and nurses were pleased that he had none of the side effects they expected him to have. He was recovering so well he was allowed to go home November 26th, one day before Thanksgiving. Before leaving the hospital, he was given the first of a series of cobalt treatments. The following Monday we began making five trips a week to NMMC in Tupelo for treatments. When the cobalt was completed, next would come chemotherapy. I kept thinking, hoping that some morning I would wake to find out this had all been a bad dream.

The time Hayes and I spent at the hospital was good. He seldom had a seizure. His mood was good, and he was almost his old self again. We laughed, talked, prayed together, took long walks up and down the corridors and enjoyed being together for the first time in almost five years. I had a peaceful, calm feeling inside that I had not known for a long, long time, which continued even after we got home. It was a wonderful feeling. My nerves were beginning to settle down. I had every hope that the tumor would be destroyed by the cobalt and chemotherapy treatments. It was wonderful to have my husband back. The Autumn colors were the most beautiful I had ever seen and each morning as we rode to Tupelo, we watched a sunrise that sent chills tingling up and down my spine. There was a crisp, cool, freshness in the air and I felt content as my husband rode beside me each day.

Hope and dreams of more years of happiness were shattered all too soon. Gradually the drug abuse began to reoccur. Hayes was slipping backward--away from me-- and no matter how hard I tried I could do nothing about it. I prayed, *"Oh God, please make him well again,"* then said hesitantly, *"if it be your will."* The hardest thing for me to do was admit and accept the fact that it may not be His Will for Hayes to be well again here on this earth. Finally, I was able to pray, *"Not my will but Thine be done. And God please give me the strength to accept whatever Your Will may be."*

On the morning of December 17, 1980, I awoke to find Hayes sleeping groggily in his recliner in the living room. In his pajama shirt pocket was a bottle of capsules containing Dilantin and phenobarbital. The same doctor who sent Hayes to Tupelo to get him straightened out had given him the prescription for these. I had been so careful to see that he took his medication exactly as it had been prescribed by the doctor in Tupelo, and now THIS! Capsules were scattered on the floor and in the chair where they had been spilled during the night. All the hurt and anger I felt before came surging back. I threw the capsules on the floor and left for school.

That day Hayes had made arrangements to ride to Tupelo with a neighbor who was also going for treatments. At noon he came to the school staggering all over the place. I was so embarrassed. When we got home that afternoon Hayes was sleeping in a drugged stupor. I told David I was leaving because I couldn't take it anymore. I left Hayes a note and went to Sarah's to spend the night. The next day David and I moved to a house on Alabama Street in New Albany which I had bought when we were separated in March. It wasn't until several weeks later I realized God had His hand in this move.

Hayes woke up about dark, found the note and called me at Sarah's house. This time he was hurt but not bitter about our leaving as he had been before. I had placed everything in God's hands at the moment I had sincerely said, *"Not my will but Thine be done."* It is for this reason I believe God was guiding us both through all the days and nights ahead.

The night I left, I went to bed early because I was exhausted, but could not go to sleep. I heard a siren going toward Myrtle. Naturally my first thought was *"Could it be?'--No it's just my nerves and I'm not going to think about it."* But it was, and at 11:00 p.m. I was at the hospital waiting for Hayes to be treated for injuries he had received in an auto accident and a broken arm sustained in a fall earlier that evening at home. He was unable to take care of himself, so I took him with me to Sarah's. She agreed to let him stay with her for a while until he could take care of himself. It turned out she was unable to take care of him so a few days later he came to stay with David and me on Alabama Street. School was out for Christmas, so I was at home every day to be with him.

Except for the overdoses of medication, the first week of Christmas vacation went relatively smoothly. He agreed to let me keep his medicine and give it to him in the correct dosage daily. A couple days later I found pills in his pocket that I recognized. I put them in the bottle with the others. This happened several times during the holidays. I couldn't figure out where he was getting them, but every time I took pills away from him, he would leave and come back with more.

Judith Ann, her two children, Ronnie and his wife and David were all home for Christmas dinner, but it was a very sad one. Hayes went to sleep in his recliner under the influence of the drugs and we couldn't get him awake to eat with us.

The week that followed Christmas was a good one in many ways. Hayes once again seemed to be doing better and several people noticed the change. We talked, laughed and joked with each other. My old Hayes had returned as much as possible for at least a while. I agreed to move back to our home in Myrtle as soon as we could do some things that needed to be done there.

Monday, January 5, 1981 was to be a day of beginnings and endings. The second semester of school was beginning. Hayes would have his last cobalt treatment and begin taking chemotherapy. There would also be an ending none of us was prepared for.

Sunday morning, January 4th Hayes, David and I went to church at Temple Baptist in Myrtle. During the afternoon Hayes decided he would ride out to Coleman's Bar-B-Q for a while. He returned home around 5:30 p.m. and went into the bathroom. Approximately 30 minutes later I heard a thud. When I got to the bathroom he was lying on the floor. I asked him what was wrong, and he just said, *"I fell."* I couldn't get him up and he was unable to help himself get up. David wasn't home so I made him as comfortable as I could, covered him with a blanket, put a pillow under his head and turned the heater on. I was afraid he would get chilled lying on the floor but there was no way I could get him up. I found pills in his pants pocket and naturally drew the conclusion he had taken an overdose and would sleep it off. When David got home at 7:30 p.m. we put Hayes to bed to do just that. I had a strange kind of gut feeling this time was different but due to past history, dismissed the thought completely.

Monday morning, January 5th, I awoke to find Hayes laying exactly the way he was when we put him to bed Sunday night. It seemed odd and made me feel very uneasy. I tried to wake him to give him his medicine but couldn't. With David's help I turned Hayes over on his side and realized his kidneys had acted during the night and the bed was wet. At this point I became very concerned. I went to Sarah's at Glenfield to call for an ambulance then she and I went back to the house.

At the hospital Hayes was given oxygen and an IV. His blood pressure was very low, and he wasn't responding to anyone. After some discussion with the doctor, he decided Hayes needed to be moved to Tupelo in case there was a blood clot or complication from the surgery. During that discussion I was told by the doctor if he pulled through this, I had no choice except to put him in an institution because he was no longer able to take care of himself and I would not be able to take care of him. The tumor and surgery had affected his reasoning and he didn't realize what he was doing to himself. On the way to Tupelo I said to Sarah, *"I can bury him easier than I can put him away somewhere to grieve for his family the rest of his life, however long that would be."*

As soon as we reached North Mississippi Medical Center a CT scan was done and no sign of blood clots on his brain were found. Immediately he was put in Intensive Care. It seemed like hours passed before the doctor finally came to give us the news---Pneumonia caused by aspiration, extremely low blood pressure, not responding to any treatment--his condition is very critical. *"If you have any children out of town, I suggest you call them,"* he said.

Ronnie, Bro. Bob and I went in to see Hayes as soon as we were allowed to. During the next visitation time we were not allowed to see him. A patient was having some problems. We found out later it was Hayes. They thought he had a light heart attack.

About 10:30 p.m. Dr. Weddle, Hayes' doctor, came to the conference room where we had all been waiting for another report. This time the news was "good". Hayes was beginning to stabilize. His condition was still very critical, but the doctor felt as if he could go home and get some rest. If we needed him the hospital would call, and he would come immediately. This was the first good news we had been given and we were all excited. We left the conference room briefly and went to the waiting room to share our good news with friends and other relatives. While we were standing there Dr. Weddle came back into the waiting room. *"Mrs. Hall,"* he said, *"could you come back into the conference room for a moment?"* I knew by the expression on his face the news was not good!

All too soon I lost my love!!!

Orville Hayes Hall
February 6, 1937–January 5, 1981

My Darling, My Dear

The words that I wrote
When our trouble first started,
Were written by one
Who was so broken hearted.

I didn't understand
The way that you felt,
What was happening inside
Wasn't your fault.

That I may be losing you
Was my greatest fear.
You were my true love,
My darling, my dear.

Now that you're gone
I miss you, oh so.
Someday I will join you
In Heaven I know.

Until the day that
Again, we can touch,
I'll love you my darling
So very, very much.

Judie Hall - 1981

If Only I Had Known

If only I had known
What I know now,
My burden would have been
So much lighter.

If only I had known
What I know now,
My concern would have been
So much greater.

In the dark I walked
For so many years.
So many of my hours
Were filled with tears.

If only I had known
What I know now,
Our life could have been
So much sweeter.

Judie Hall - 1981

The Knot in Life's Rope

When trouble surrounds you
And no one to care;
There's hope in the Master,
Your burdens He'll share.

Life seems to be slipping,
You've almost lost hope;
Christ is the answer,
The knot in life's rope.

When the end you have reached,
Just keep hanging on;
Remember that God
Gave His only Son,

And all who will ask Him
With problems to cope,
Find Jesus the knot
In the end of life's rope.

Judie Hall - 1981

Made in the USA
Columbia, SC
25 March 2024